Sketches of Nebraska

Robert Hanna

Sketches of Nebraska

For Nancy —
with all my best
Robert Hanna
January 1988

UNIVERSITY OF NEBRASKA PRESS   LINCOLN AND LONDON

Library of Congress Cataloging
in Publication Data

Hanna, Robert, 1939-
Sketches of Nebraska.

1. Hanna, Robert, 1939-
2. Nebraska in art.
3. Nebraska — Description
and travel.   I. Title.
NC139.H27A4 1984   741.943   84-3722
ISBN 0-8032-2328-5 (alk. paper)

SECOND PRINTING: 1985

For Arlene and our children, Laura, Robert, and Lisa

Preface

On the wintry night of February 9, 1939, my mother was unable to get to a hospital in O'Neill or Neligh, Nebraska, because the roads were impassable. There was no hospital in my little home town of Ewing, and with the assistance of my Uncle Louie, Mother gave birth to twin boys in an apartment above a beer tavern. Both of the babies appeared to be dead, but soon one cried out. My brother, Roger, died without taking a breath. As the surviving twin, I'm still possessed by the events of that evening, although my Uncle Louie took forty years to tell me what had happened. Mother died without speaking of it. Each time I pass through Ewing, I stand before that tavern storefront and wonder at the balance of joy and grief that my mother must have experienced that night now long ago.

In nearly all small towns, wherever they may be, the beer taverns are survivors too. The one below my birthplace is still doing business. Sitting at the bar and looking across the street to the place where the outdoor dance floor and bandshell used to be, I can still see the strings of electric lights that once draped excitement and dazzle across those summer evenings. So much of what I remember of Ewing is gone — the Eldorado Theater, the Green Lantern Cafe, the Splitter Brothers Store, and the creamery.

Those losses are a big part of this sketchbook. A building torn down, a dance floor obliterated — to a person living in Ewing these changes have happened so gradually that they've hardly been noticed, and for a generation or two the memories of familiar places stand as sturdily in the mind's eye as do the landmarks themselves. And then, slowly, they begin to fade.

Ewing, Nebraska, is like hundreds of small towns across the United States. And time and change make their erasures everywhere. But for me, the town of Ewing is my personal metaphor for change and loss, and with the scratching of my pen I've tried to preserve my recollections of a place and time now gone forever.

In 1943, my parents moved our family to Grand Island, hoping to secure a better education for their children. Our family of five moved into a three-room bungalow near the foot of the west overpass into the city. This serpentine concrete bridge was the west entrance into Grand Island, and it lifted the highway up and over the Union Pacific tracks, where the great steam locomotives roared through, pulling long trains of supplies for survival and war. In many ways, this overpass resembles a Roman aqueduct, and when I was young it was lined with lanterns on standards with large globes of glass. It was a noble introduction to the city, and I've done many drawings of this structure, though the lanterns are gone and the overpass has begun to crumble away.

My childhood in Grand Island was a happy one, and the family's occasional trips back to Ewing on Highway 281 were particularly joyful, as we sat wedged together in our black 1941 Ford, laughing and talking. I watched Nebraska pass by from my seat by the rear window, and slowly my interest in the landscape began to develop. It was a four-hundred-mile round trip to Ewing and back, and I got to see a lot of Nebraska. I picked out my own set of landmarks to watch for—a big stand of cottonwoods north of Bartlett, the bridge over the Loup at St. Paul, the night lights at the U.S. Army airfield north of Grand Island, the watermelon stands at St. Libory, and the bright red Rooney elevator in Greeley.

I learned to draw at an early age, and my grade school teachers were so impressed with my skill that they excused me from music class so that I could draw scenic and seasonal landscapes for the school bulletin boards. Although it was wonderful to be excused from singing and its embarrassments, I had to pay for the privilege by standing in as a silent palm tree in the annual Christmas plays.

My favorite subjects for drawing were not, however, the acceptable leafy autumn and snowy winter landscapes my teachers urged on me. I preferred to spend my time detailing World War II aircraft, pictures of elaborate bat-

viii

tles, studies of Indians and their encampments. I was convinced that there were Indians still living in tepees in the hills around Ewing and Clearwater, and I did what I could to authenticate these imaginary people by drawing them.

Growing up in Grand Island seemed to me one big expedition. I pedaled my two-toned, cream and black Schwinn over every inch of the town, displaying its baseball decals for all the world to see. I whizzed from Webb's livestock yards on the west side over to the Union Pacific yards on the east. The old livestock company is still there, but with the decline of the railroads the U.P. shops were no longer needed, and the wonderful brick roundhouse was razed in the sixties. I can still envision those magnificent steam locomotives filling that grand building with their black and oily power.

The railroad split Grand Island into the north side and the south side, and the tracks forming the dividing line became my playground. It was along the shiny rails that we played hide and seek in the evenings and helped to unload the Barnum and Bailey circus train when it rolled in once each summer. When it was chilly, we warmed ourselves at the depot. A special rendezvous in all weather was the corner drugstore at Fourth and Walnut. It had a soda fountain with green wicker seats and a marble counter top. From the soda fountain we could see the most familiar landmark of my boyhood, the tall smokestack of the old power plant, which towered over every adventure we had. I've put this smokestack in many of my drawings, and just seeing it there on the horizon makes me feel secure.

My bike, decorated with the Ted Williams decals, also took me to the swimming pool on the south side and the ice skating pond at the Old Soldiers' and Sailors' Home on the north. The town was just the right size for me. I grew familiar with every nook and cranny of the downtown area while I was selling the *Grand Island Independent* on street corners. I came to know every alley, every place of business front and back, and every little cul de sac along my route. Those places and spaces became a part of me, and I've done drawings of them all in my attempt to keep them fresh in my memory.

The main corner where I sold papers hasn't changed much at all, and the Coney Island Lunch Room is still on my list of stops when I go back to visit. Across the street from the Coney was Wolbach's Department Store, and there I made spending money as a window trimmer. I also did illustrations for the newspaper while I was in high school. Working on the window displays was fun, but drawing salt and pepper shakers for the newspaper ads was hard work, particularly since I've yet to master the art of drawing glass. Not far from the store was the Yancey Hotel, the highest building in town. When I wished, I could climb the back stairs up through all eleven of its stories and from the top could get a view of the great Platte River to the south and east.

On Saturday nights the stores were open until nine, and all of the farmers came to town to visit and shop. My parents were good about letting me stay out at night, and I was always downtown looking around. I recall a sidewalk vendor named Arthur who had a hot tamale wagon that filled the streets with spicy aromas. I remember the farm wives sitting in their cars, calling back and forth to each other. I remember the men standing in clusters, storying and spitting and occasionally taking a cautious sip out of the mouth of a paper bag. Some women would drive their cars into town in the middle of the day just to get a good spot on the main street. Then they'd return home on the tractors that their husbands had followed them in with. That night, the husband and wife would come back on the tractor and she would get out and occupy her seat in the car. I once asked a friend what had happened to those days and she replied, "Parking meters."

My art teachers influenced me a great deal. In high school, Mr. Carl Wegener worked hard to encourage me. I was fortunately able to pair off with a friend, Jack Hughes, who has since become an artist and teacher of art. The two of us would work at drawing and painting together. When we

x

were late for our next class, we could always get Mr. Wegener to write an excuse for us. And in the summer he took us out to the Platte River to draw. The bridges along that river still charm me. As a boy I secretly jumped from the railroad bridge—a feat that no one else would have been stupid enough to attempt—where the rails cross the river at the old Central Power Plant. That bridge is still standing, and I've sketched it many times, but there's not a brick left of the power plant.

Carl Wegener also gave me a copy of the classic treatise *Space, Time, and Architecture,* and although I couldn't understand it at the time, it was my first introduction to architecture, the field I eventually chose as my own. I applied for assistance at the University of Nebraska and received the Leo A. Daly four-year architecture scholarship. Without it, I would not have been able to attend college.

One of the reasons I got the scholarship was not talent, but costume. I wore my best short-sleeved shirt to the interview and found to my embarrassment that all of the other applicants were dressed in suits and ties. I was the last one to be interviewed, and the wait seemed to last forever. When I was ushered into the office of the chairman, I discovered that he too was wearing a short-sleeved shirt. We hit it off immediately.

Sketching and perspective drawing were taught in the Department of Architecture, and I learned that every good architect could sketch and draw well. Drawing was the method by which one expressed ideas and conveyed design concepts. The drawings of famous architects like Bertram Goodhue, Schell Lewis, and Frank Lloyd Wright fascinated me, and I wanted to be able to draw as well as they had.

It was from a professor at the university, Patrick Horsburgh, that I acquired the idea of using drawings to record the passing scene in Nebraska. His drawings of places he'd visited were marvelous. His class assignments included photographing and sketching places of architectural or historical significance. He believed that sketching deepened one's sense of selectivity and observation and made one more sensitive to one's surroundings. He also held that history and its effects are ever present and inescapable. The thought of doing a Nebraska sketchbook has been with me since those days, when he awakened me to the history and architecture of this state.

Two other situations during my college days heightened my awareness of my surroundings. During one year, I commuted between Lincoln and Grand Island weekly by bus or train. The bus rides down old Highway 34 familiarized me with particular landscapes in just the way the trips between Grand Island and Ewing had. The bus stopped in every town—Seward, Utica, York, Bradshaw, Hampton, Aurora—and passed over the Hamilton County bridge on the Platte. I'd slept under that bridge one night during a rainstorm and I was fond of its rhythmic arches.

The train ride back to Lincoln was a night trip. I would leave at three-thirty in the morning and get to the capital city by six o'clock, ready for breakfast. I couldn't see much of the landscape during those hours and I was mainly working at staying warm on the unheated train, but I did watch the distant farm lights and the lights of towns and attempted to imagine what sort of buildings slept there in the darkness, the soft light of the single bulbs illuminating their gray faces. My memories of the depots in Grand Island and Lincoln are vivid to this day, and I've sketched those buildings many times.

At one point in my college career, Robert Douglass, a classmate, and I lived as guests in the Ames mansion in Lincoln. It was a lovely old Queen Anne home owned by Mrs. Grace Ames. Entering the grounds on South Twentieth Street was like leaving the twentieth century. There was a whole world of sketches to be done of that place, which has since been destroyed.

My degree in architecture and my registration as an architect led me to a private practice that has continued since 1968. Those many years of practice have meant dozens of meetings with building committees for schools, churches, banks, city councils, and individuals. I travel with a sketchbook and make quick notations as I go. Often these sketches are among the best things that come from such a meeting. Driving the state's highways and byways to attend those discussions, I've realized how much of Nebraska has been lost and how much must be saved.

The sketchbook is the artist's notebook, his journal, in which he records his observations in the language that he knows best — that of shape and line and contrast. Drawing is the handwriting of the visual artist, and each sketch reveals the artist as he discusses with himself the experiences that each day brings.

The drawings that appear in this book cover a span of many years, and were drawn because the scenes represented and the drawings as they came from my pen were of substantial interest to me. Sometimes, through the miracle of drawing, something more interesting emerges in a drawing than existed in the subject. These sketches portray Nebraska, as it was in the past and as it remains today. Many of the buildings represented here are now gone. I looked at them once, scratched out my drawing, and when I looked back they had disappeared — destroyed by fire or weather or the wrecking crew. Only my sketches and the memories of local townspeople persist to substantiate the existence of many of the places you'll see in these pages, and these pages struggle hard to capture a passing scene that I hold dear.

The subjects of the various drawings may appear to be rather ordinary. Most of the structures do not have architectural or historical importance to anyone but me and those whose lives, like mine, have been touched by them. The people of Nebraska are fortunate to have access to hundreds of photographs of the great landmarks of our state — the opera houses, grand hotels, town halls, county courthouses. These photographs are as near as the corner library. But what I have always been irresistibly drawn to are those buildings that nobody notices — the roadside diner, the gas station, the simple neighborhood bungalow. These were the structures about which I played as a boy, and about which I stroll in my imagination today. This book is about what Nebraska means to me, one man who grew up there, and I've tried to make it a work of reverence.

The drawings are a selection from the hundreds I've made over the years. My criteria for selection have been threefold: I have chosen, first, those drawings that I like best, those that seem artistically superior. Next, I've selected drawings which portray the originality and vitality and strength of Nebraska's carpenters, architects, builders, and engineers. Finally, I've included drawings of buildings which are at the time of this writing standing in the shade of the wrecking crane. Perhaps by calling attention to some of these magnificent and irreplaceable structures, I can help to preserve them.

I've made lots of what I call "windshield tours" of the towns in my state. I've driven up and down those Main Streets and Front Streets and First Streets, and I've been on most of the back streets, too. I've been out of my white station wagon as much as I've been in it, and I've walked through alleys and the aisles of little department stores. I've rocked on the edges of hundreds of vinyl-topped stools, and eaten fine slabs of berry and pumpkin and green tomato pie in cafés from one end of the state to the other. Nebraska is my state, a place with vitality and vastness and variety, and in pursuit of subjects for these drawings I now offer, I've had the perfect opportunity to "loaf and invite my soul," as Walt Whitman wrote.

Illustrations

Sketches of Nebraska

1. Old water tower, Ewing

2. Beer tavern, author's birthplace, Ewing

3. The El Dorado Theater (razed 1973), Ewing

4. The Green Lantern Cafe (razed 1971), Ewing

5. Cottonwood and St. Peters Catholic Church, Ewing

6. Watermelon stand, Highway 281, St. Libory

7. The Rooney Elevator, Greeley

8. Highway 30 overpass, Grand Island

9. Webb's Livestock Yards, Grand Island

10. Union Pacific Railroad roundhouse (razed 1966), Grand Island

11. Old Union Pacific baggage depot (razed 1968), Grand Island

12. Walnut Drug, (closed early 1960s), 4th and Walnut, Grand Island

13. Pine Street power plant, Grand Island

14. Union Pacific and Burlington watchtower (razed 1983), Grand Island

15. The Coney Island Lunch Room, Grand Island

16. Railroad bridge over the Platte, Hall County

Robert Hanna

17. Hall County courthouse, Grand Island

18. Horse stables, Saddleclub (destroyed by 1980 tornado), Grand Island

Robert Hanna

19. Barn group, Highway 34, Seward County

20. Hayrack, Highway 34, Seward County

Robert Hanna

21. Miers Brothers Livestock, Seward

22. Cattle chutes and elevators, York

23. Railroad crossing, Seward County

24. Abandoned barn, York County

25. Abandoned elevator, Houston, York County

26. Ebenezer Church, south of Waco

Robert Hanna
1976

27. York County courthouse (razed 1977), York

28. Elevator (partially razed 1983), south of York

29. The town hall, Bradshaw

30. Small barn, York County

31. Hamilton County courthouse, Aurora

32. Hampton Co-op elevator, Hampton

33. Hamilton County bridge over the Platte

34. Union Pacific Railroad depot, Grand Island

35. Burlington Railroad depot, Grand Island

36. Switching yard, west Lincoln

37. Burlington Railroad yard, Lincoln

38. The Ames residence (razed 1965), Lincoln

39. Green Valley Cafe (abandoned) on Highway 6, Funk

40. Salem Episcopal Methodist Church, near Axtell

Robert Hanna

41. Old Platte River bridge, Kearney

42. Old trolley car barns, Kearney

43. Union Pacific depot (moved to Shelton 1974), Gibbon

44. Old Ford dealership, Shelton

Robert Hanna

45. Union Pacific Railroad depot, Gibbon

46. Grain elevators, Doniphan

47. Country mailboxes, Kearney County

48. Main Street, Heartwell

49. Grain elevator, Norman

50. Radford round barn, north of Minden

51. Old First National Bank, Minden

52. Livery stable, Warp's Pioneer Village, Minden

53. Zion Lutheran chapel, Bethphage Mission, Axtell

54. The Carpenter house, near Lowell

55. Railroad depot and Otto Elevator, Charleston, York County

56. Water tower standpipe, Henderson

57. The Updike Elevator, Gresham

58. The Jeffery homestead, near Benedict

59. Country bridge, York County

60. Railroad depot and grain elevator, McCool Junction

61. Barns, east of Exeter

62. Fillmore County courthouse, Geneva

63. Grain elevator, Denton

64. Burlington Railroad crossing, Crete

65. Grain elevator, Wymore

66. Railroad water tower, Wymore

67. Old DeWitt Flour Mill, DeWitt

68. Hotel Wilber, Wilber

69. Railroad depot, Wymore

70. McClure barn, Roca

71. Traubel's popcorn stand, Beatrice

72. Cemetery, Highway 77, near Beatrice

73. Old elevator (razed 1973), west of Lincoln

74. Old Rock Island depot (now Union Bank and Trust Company), Lincoln

75. Yankee Hill brickyard, Lincoln

76. Monk's Cafe (razed 1973), Lincoln

77. Old Telephone Exchange Building, Lincoln

78. Maple Lodge (Robert Allington residence), Lincoln

79. Old barn, near Greenwood

80. Country bridge over railroad, Highway 6, Cass County

81. Cottonwoods, south of Ceresco

82. Rock Creek railroad bridge (razed 1983), north of Ceresco

83. Railroad depot, Wahoo

84. The Wigwam Cafe, Wahoo

Robert Hanna

85. Farm Structures, Cass County

86. Corn crib, Cass County

Robert Hanna

87. Country bridge and abandoned railroad, near Alvo

88. Old house, Highway 63, north of Ashland

89. Corn crib, Cass County

90. Old tree and farmyard, Cass County

91. Grain elevator, St. Edward

92. Country barn, Nance County

93. Village view, Raeville

Robert Hanna

94. St. Bonaventure's Catholic Church, Raeville

95. Richard Zeilinger residence, David City

96. Farmyard near Columbus

97. Union Pacific Railroad depot (razed 1981), Clarks

98. Wagner Mills Elevator (destroyed by fire 1983), Columbus

99. Old elevator and Neligh Mill, Neligh

100. Barn, Dodge County

101. Country school (abandoned), Highway 73, north of Auburn

102. Old shingle house, Falls City

103. The Minick house, Brownville

104. The Minick house, Brownville

105. Old brick house, Brownville

106. The Beehive, Brownville

107. The Tipton house (Smith residence), Brownville

108. Bridge at Brownville

Robert Hanna

109. Merrywood on the Missouri, Brownville

110. Bridge over the Missouri, Brownville

111. Pedestrian walkway and Burlington Railroad depot, McCook

112. Farm structures, Red Willow County

113. Kearney County courthouse, Minden

114. Main Street, Greeley

Within the illustration: VALENTINE ¼ MI., PRANGS APPAREL

Robert Hanna

115. Sign to Valentine, Highway 83, Cherry County

116. View of the Niobrara River, near Valentine

Robert Hanna

117. Sale barn (abandoned), Bartley

118. The Beman ranch, near Springview

119. Gas station and cafe (abandoned), Sutton

Robert Hanna

120. Roadside cafe (razed 1972), Highway 30, Schuyler

121. Grain elevator (razed 1981), Sheldonville

122. St. Anselm Catholic Church, Anselmo

123. Thiessen barn, Clearwater

124. My mother, Lola's, country school, Antelope County, near Clearwater